THE BABY EXERCISE BOOK

For the First Fifteen Months

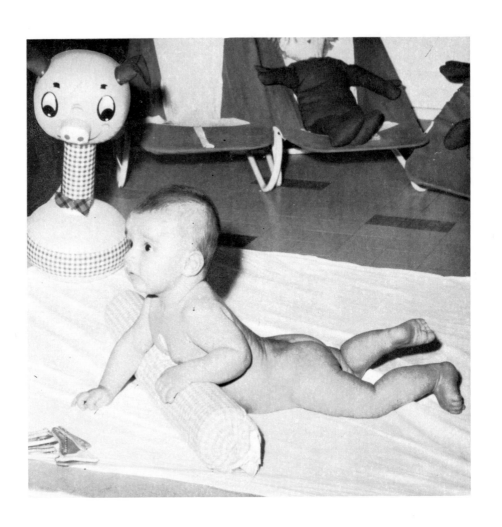

THE
BABY EXERCISE
BOOK

For the First Fifteen Months

Updated and Expanded Edition

by Dr. Janine Lévy

Translated from the French by Eira Gleasure

Pantheon Books
A Division of Random House
New York

Revised material translated by Dr. Hermina Benjamin.
Copyright © 1975 by Random House, Inc.

Preface Copyright © 1973 by Random House, Inc.

English translation Copyright © 1973 by William Collins Sons & Co. Ltd.

Library of Congress Cataloging in Publication Data

Lévy, Janine.
The Baby Exercise Book: For the First Fifteen Months.

Translation of *L'éveil du tout-petit.*
1. Infants—Care and hygiene. 2. Exercise—
Physiological effect. I. Title. [DNLM: 1. Infant
care. 2. Movement—In infancy and childhood. WS113
L668e].
RJ61.L55313 1975   649'.57   75-10590
ISBN 0-394-73122-0

3456789B

Design by Sheila Lynch

Preface

The arrival of a baby brings striking changes in the lives of his parents. The newborn becomes the center of their attention and carefully, often anxiously, they follow his progress day by day, to be sure that all is well.

A mother's natural desire to love and care for her newborn child is sometimes mixed with doubts. She may be uncertain about how much to touch her baby and how much motion she should stimulate. Child-rearing practices vary widely with culture and socioeconomic status, and are often contradictory, as is much advice the young mother will receive from friends and relatives.

Physicians who specialize in child development are unanimous about one point: the more interaction between parents and child the better for the child. This interaction forms the cornerstone of emotional stability later in life. In addition, the more a mother touches and plays with her child, the more she will learn about him and the better able she will be to recognize any unusual behavior.

For a long time it was generally accepted that the development of movement by a child was an invariant process. It was thought to be based entirely on reflex activity, which depends upon the maturation of the nervous system. This meant that crawling, walking, and other activities could not be influenced by the actions of others. This view is changing, however. It is now thought that factors other than reflexes are responsible for the child's motor development. He can learn, for example, by copying those close to him. Often people say that a youngster behaves or moves just like his father, or that in certain activities he imitates his mother.

Children have an inborn drive to move. A newborn baby lying awake on his back is constantly moving. Furthermore, certain methods of stimulation can bring out certain patterns of movement. For instance, if a newborn lies on his stomach on a flat surface like a bed and you press the soles of his feet with your hands, he will initiate some crawling movements. He will make sideward movements with his spine and draw his legs close to his body alternately, moving away from the support given to his feet. If you continue to push against his soles to give some support for a pushoff, the baby will continue to crawl.

Reports about children's development always refer to the walking reflex, placing reflex, and grasping relfex. A reflex response is only one component of a purposeful activity, which is the result of the learning and integration of many individual motor activities.

Motor development in babies varies. One starts to walk earlier than another, and the child who walks later is not necessarily abnormal. If you stimulate your child frequently, he or she will not necessarily walk sooner than the child next door. Some investigators[1] have demonstrated, however, that children who are encouraged or assisted start to walk earlier, on the average, than their contemporaries who had no stimulation at all. There is also some evidence that there is some relationship between physical activity and the development of the nervous system.

It is well established that the motor nerves, which enable us to move and contract the muscles, are not fully developed until the age of four or five and sometimes even later. Physical stimulation by adults, however, does help the child to develop earlier such motor skills as coordination. Early mobility inspires confidence and develops visual, spatial, and tactile impressions of the environment. Mobility and some motor skill in touching and handling objects help the infant to satisfy his intellectual curiosity and the drive to seek and explore. They give the infant more competence to perform a desired activity.[2]

This book serves as a good guideline for parents who want to facilitate motor activity in newborns and infants. There is no danger of overstimulation. The activities and exercises are staged in four groups, according to age. Parents should not feel compelled to adhere closely to these, for from the first day of life, humans vary in the rate of their development. This book should help to smooth the road to the development of all the wonderful potentials humans are endowed with at birth.

June, 1973   WILLIBALD NAGLER, M.D., F.A.C.P.
                                 Chief, Rehabilitation Medicine
                                 The New York Hospital-Cornell Medical Center

[1] P. R. Zelazo, N. A. Zelazo, S. Kolb, *Science* 176 (1972): 314–15.
[2] R. White, *Psychological Review* 66 (1959): 297.

Acknowledgments

We wish to thank particularly:
Dr. Elsbeth Kong of Berne for her introduction to methods of exercising the whole body.

Mlle. Danièle Rapoport, psychologist, and Mme. Yette Tabusse, kinestherapist, for the many suggestions they have made.

Michèle Fory, Dijana Tissier, kinestherapist, and Josette Intartaglia, for the help and support they have given to us.

Anne-Marie Zurbach and Philippe Lévy, photographers whose patience and kindness have overcome the difficulties of working with children.

We also wish to thank:
la Direction générale de l'Action sanitaire et sociale de Paris, who have shown their confidence in us and made their establishments available to us, the chief medical officer of the Protection maternelle et infantile, who has given us his advice and criticism,

the principals, child welfare assistants, and all the staff of the Paris crèches, who have made us so welcome and with whom we have had so much pleasure in working,

and also the parents of the children photographed.

CONTENTS

HOW TO USE THIS BOOK

Make sure you understand all the exercises, practice on the rag doll, then close the book. Play with your child: a spontaneous movement from him is much better than an impeccable technique with no response.

Introduction

This book, which is the result of long experience, was published with the intention of offering parents and educators a method of developing self-awareness in infants and very young children through their movements.

Its writing was prompted by the question: Should we leave to chance, instinct, or the inspiration of the moment the task of initiating, reinforcing, and correcting the motor achievements of the child?—when it is possible, in an atmosphere of play and security, to take advantage of all opportunities to give the child the means to progress and acquire self-reliance.

We can prepare him to master the sitting position by strengthening his muscles, standing up by making him aware of the role and support of his feet, walking by facilitating his search for balance. This does not mean restraining him, even less pushing him. It means keeping pace with his own rhythm and personality, to assist his progress in controlling his body and help his all-around development by making him feel at ease in his own body.

This modification—minimal and fundamental—in the upbringing of a child is desirable and possible right here and now. It requires neither money nor time. But it requires a radical change in our habits, a shift in the attitude of the parents or their substitutes.

This change should pervade all the actions of everyday life: the method of carrying the child, changing him, washing him, feeding him, and playing with him. Every "situation" should be turned to advantage in encouraging and stimulating the child's spontaneous activity by talking to him, explaining what is expected of him, and prompting his participation. We do this by interfering as little as possible, by not disturbing his spontaneous activity, by giving him time to change position, by prolonging the movements he tries, and by allowing him to discover and explore his most beautiful toy: his body.

Such a practice—as our everyday experience has proven—helps to achieve surprising results in both normal and retarded infants. Not only does it prevent deformities and correct bad posture, but it consolidates his motor achievements and thus contributes to his balance and diminishes his fears. It gives him the invaluable feeling of security. It also gives an added attraction to the role of parent or nurse. Thus the "development game" of body contact, loving exchanges, and reciprocal gratifications enriches the adult-child relationship and deepens the parent-infant symbiosis.

We must also mention that the latest research in neurophysiology brings to our intuition, to our daily experience of contact with children, the theoretical basis and the scientific explanation which was missing.

The post-natal maturation of the central nervous system in infants not only is remarkable in its importance, but takes a long time. If the effects on the organization of the cerebral cortex of an environment rich in stimuli are still debated, one thing is certain: the infant's sensitivity to the physical, social, and cultural conditions of the environment.

Therefore, it is no longer enough to love and feed the child. We must understand and know that his motor activities contribute to the development of his brain, that they are indispensable for the organization of his nervous system. Deprived of these stimuli, it loses its inborn functions.

For purposes of simplification, we will consider four phases of the child's motor development:

First phase up to three months: the period in which the movement education will be based essentially on relaxation.

Second phase from three to six months: the period of gymnastics in preparation for the sitting position.

Third phase from six to twelve months: the period of all-round movement, mastering the sitting position, and preparing for the standing position.

Fourth phase from nine to fifteen months (and beyond): the period of playing, mastering the standing position, and preparation for movement independence.

A wide range of movements corresponds to each of these phases. Everyone should feel free to choose and adapt from the movements those which best suit a specific child and the person who takes care of him. They should be accompanied by talk, song, rhythm, and music in a calm and relaxed atmosphere. The child will quickly respond to verbal stimulation, encouragement, the slightest gesture and tone of voice. He will hope for and anticipate your reactions, your smiles.

We hope that this book, in its simple presentation, will help you and increase your confidence. We think that it will bring to the child something essential for his motor, intellectual, and affective fulfillment.

THE BABY EXERCISE BOOK

For the First Fifteen Months

2 materials

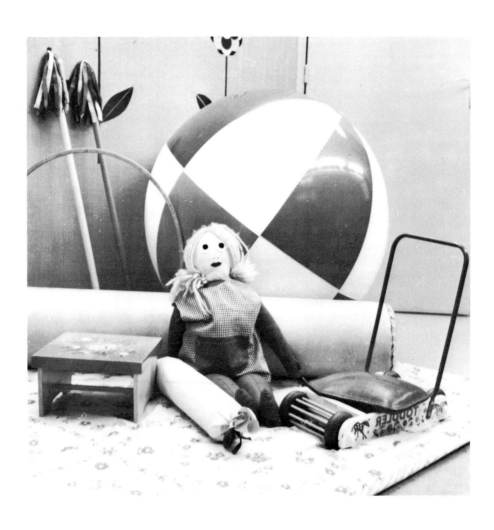

Two tapering cushions, stuffed with kapok or cut from foam rubber (see sketches): one 2 inches high, the other 3 inches high, depending on the child's size. (See page 29.) Alternative—use a rolled-up towel.

Two cylindrical cushions: one 7 inches in diameter by 24 inches in length, the other 10 inches in diameter by 40 inches in length.

To make these cushions: cover a cardboard mailing tube with a sheet of foam rubber of the right thickness to obtain the required diameter; put paper cement along the long edges of the sheet; leave to dry; stick the edges onto each other by rolling the sheet of foam around the cardboard tube; cover the finished cylinder with washable material or plastic.

cushions

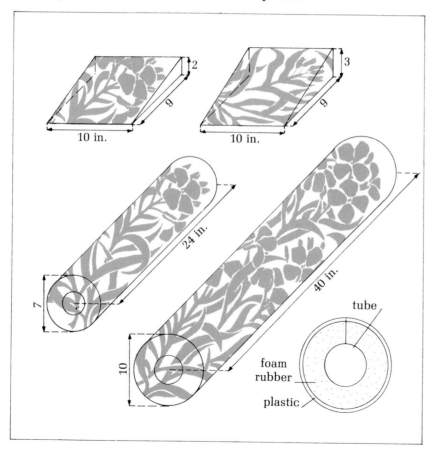

4   **A rag doll** the size of a one-year-old baby, to help you to learn how to handle a child's body and develop freedom of movement (see pattern below).

A large beach ball about 31 inches in diameter, slightly deflated. Alternative —use the mother's knees or stomach.

Rods (broom handles covered with contact paper; decorate these with little ribbons or bells) for preparing the child to walk unaided.

A baby-walker on wheels whose handle must reach the child's shoulder. Load it with a weight equivalent to the child's: to help him to walk. Alternative—use a kitchen stool.

A hoop for helping him to learn to walk, changing from crouching to standing position, dancing around. Alternative—use a belt.

pattern for the doll

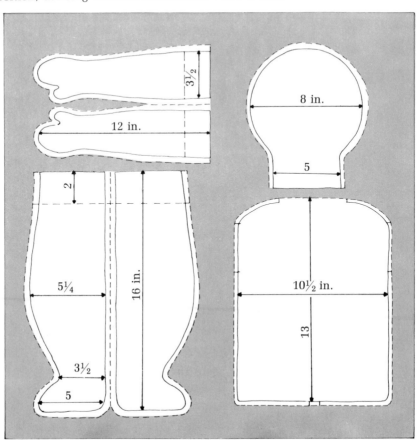

A backless wooden stool, 5 to 5½ inches high, whose seat is about 12 to 14 inches across. Alternative—use dictionaries.

A mirror: the child will see himself, recognize himself, and be able to understand his own movements and gestures. Put it 12 inches from the ground. It must be large enough for you to be able to see and control his movements.

A table about 3 feet 9 inches wide covered with foam rubber, or a foam rubber mat 1¼ inches thick, 5½ feet on each side, covered with plastic material. Alternative—a blanket on the ground.

Various toys, according to the child's age. *An airy room,* with a temperature of 69 ° to 71 °F (20 to 22 °C).

**rag
doll**

FIRST PHASE:
up to three months

During this period the newborn baby's life is interrupted by sleep and feedings in a pattern that he comes to expect. From this age on, each child's personality begins to evolve. Some are very lively, others are slow to react. But all need to be cuddled, spoken to gently, stimulated, and to move.

What can you do with your baby?

Relaxing: At this age this is most important. The young infant's body is very tense, with arms and legs bent and fists clenched. After exercises for general and local relaxation, the limbs and body will loosen up: the child will sleep better, and cry less. You can do these relaxing exercises after bathtime, but before night. Exercising too late may make your baby cry too long. Five or ten minutes should be long enough for these movements.

Some gymnastic movements: The term gymnastics may seem unsuitable, for these movements are really muscular reflexes in response to stimulation. But if there is encouragement with each stimulation, and if each time the child responds you show your pleasure in your face, gestures, and voice, the child will very quickly understand what you want. Communication has begun. This reflex response, at first only involuntary, will very quickly become the voluntary response you are expecting. These few movements will develop depth of breathing, aid digestion, regularize bowel movements, and tone up the abdominal wall.

A movement involving the whole body: Turn him over and back again.

What you should know

All children need calm and routine, and the best pattern should be found for each child.

Avoid sudden, quick, or jerky movements. Get used to the exercises by using a rag doll at first; practice in front of a mirror to get perfect control over your actions.

You can make it possible for your child to relax only if you yourself are relaxed and at ease. These exercises are not compulsory. This is not work: you must want to play with your child, and enjoy this shared pleasure.

Advice for day-to-day routine

How should the child be carried? Carry him sometimes on your right arm, sometimes on your left; the child's head and body should be fully supported. Very early you can have him sit on your thigh with knees and chest supported and face away from you.

How should he be laid down? Change his position frequently during the day. Put the child on one side, then the other, flat on his back, or on his tummy. This latter position is recommended from his first weeks (put him completely flat to sleep). He will very quickly lift his head and so will begin to strengthen the muscles of his back and neck. As his hands are busy feeling the ground, his thumb will be less likely to find its way to his mouth, a favorite pastime with children who lie habitually flat on their backs.

How should he be spoken to? Stand very close to the child when you talk to him, and sometimes sing softly. Prepare him, explain to him what you plan to do from the very first days.

What toys should he have? A shiny mobile above his crib, a loud-sounding musical rattle, brightly colored balls strung across the crib. Don't change them, always put them in the same place. This way the child will find them faster.

What environment should he have? As the newborn child sleeps a lot, the crib will be his preferred spot. While awake, put him on a foam rubber mat.

How should he be cared for? Move him gently, avoid fast changes of position, always support his head. Extend the slightest movement he tries.

relaxation of the whole body

Position: Put the naked child flat on his back on a
slightly deflated ball or on a table covered
with foam rubber.

 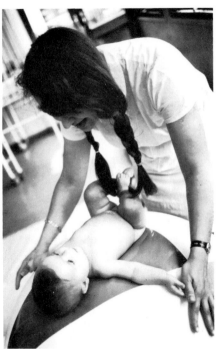

By patting slowly, regularly, and very softly, either on
the ball or directly on the child, you should obtain total
relaxation of the body (arms, legs, neck, and back).

Note: The child should be naked, as only the direct contact
between his skin and the ball gives the necessary
adherence. Make sure you stimulate and then wait for
the child's reactions.

Aim: To familiarize the child with the ball. To let
him get to know it by sight and touch, in order to
avoid all feelings of insecurity when it is used later.

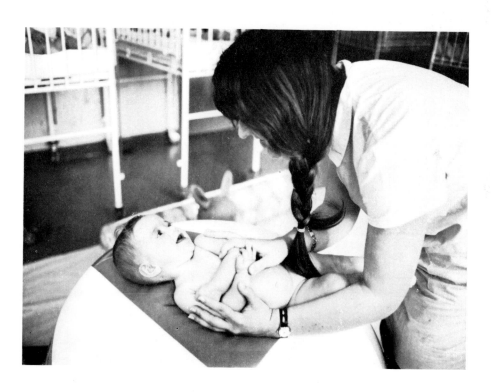

opening the hand

Position: The child lying flat on his back on the ground or on a table covered with a foam rubber sheet.

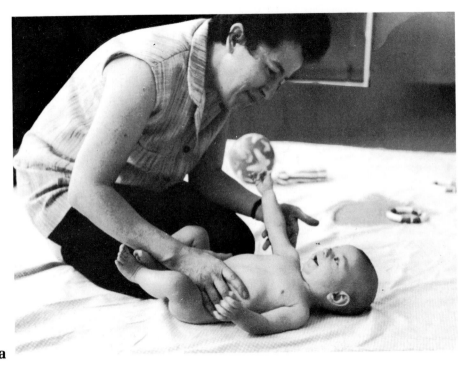

a

Begin the loosening-up at shoulder level **(a),** making regular pats, progress along to the hand **(b).** Toss the arm gently up and down **(c).** When the child has opened his hand, relax the other arm and hand; make him stroke his body and face, then yours and your hand.

Note: Take hold of his arm in the
middle of the long bones; never tug
it—this could pull it out of joint.
You must wait for the muscles to
relax. Your own hand and
arm must be very flexible.

Aim: To make the hand open by
relaxing the shoulder.

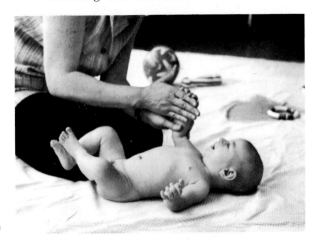

b

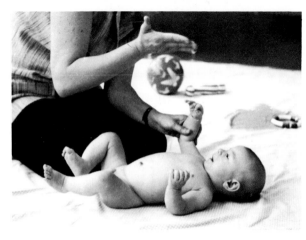

c

the scarf exercise

Position: The child lying flat on his back on the ground
or on a table.

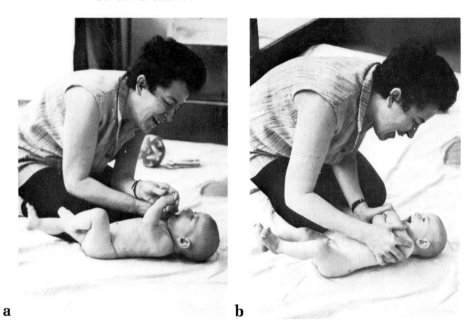

a   b

With arms crossed grip the child's forearms **(a).** Draw the
hands gently toward the opposite shoulders, using the
relaxing movement just described **(b).** Let the child feel his
body, stroke his shoulder, chest, and face.

Note: Always watch the way you hold his arms and the
gentleness of your movements.

Aim: Awareness of the body. Relaxation.

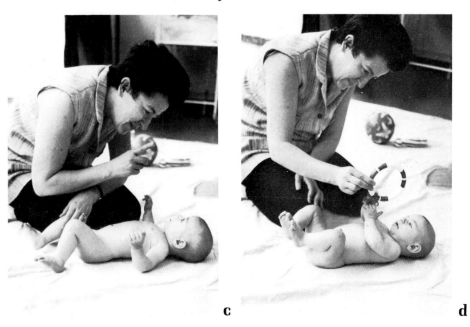

c   d

Gently let go of the child's hands **(c).** Hold a toy out to him
(d). Let him stroke it and look at it: one day he will take it.

relaxing the arms

Position: The child flat on his back on the ground,
the ball, or the table.

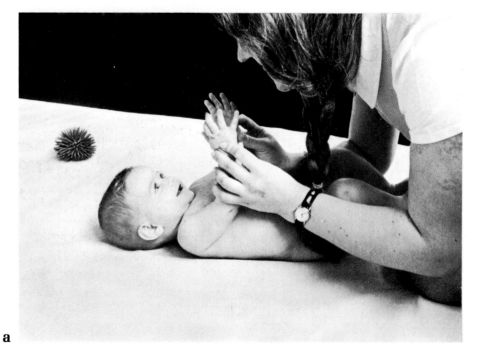

a

Let the child take hold of your thumbs or hold him by
his forearms: stretch his arms forward **(a).** Lower
them sideways in the form of a cross **(b).**

Note: The arms must be completely extended at shoulder level and drawn carefully into the cross position.

Aim: To extend the arms completely.

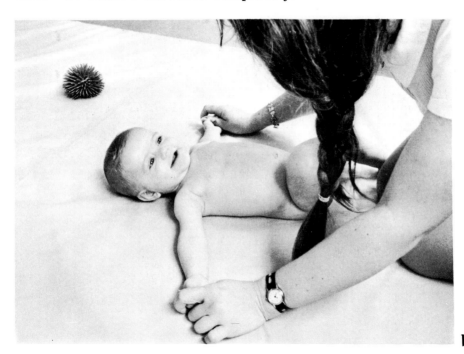

b

relaxing the legs

Position: The child flat on his back, on the ground or
on the table.

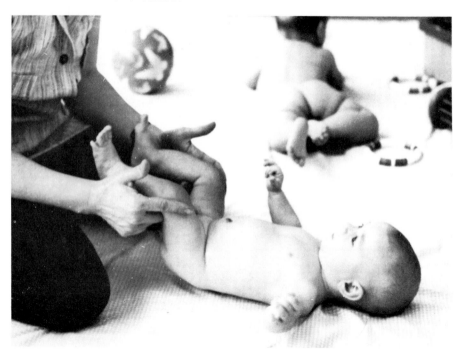

Support both legs under the knee joint, and toss them
gently up and down.

Aim: To extend the legs and stretch out the muscles.

Alternatively, by patting and tossing, move one knee up
to the chest, and then the other.

straightening out the legs

Position: The child flat on his back, on the ground or on the table, legs together.

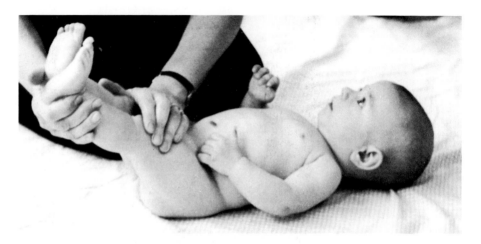

With one hand under the child's calves, the other on his knees, gently draw the legs out into a horizontal position.

Note: Watch the position of the pelvis. The whole lumbar region should be in contact with the surface of the table. Never go beyond the child's capabilities. The bent lower limbs will straighten quite normally in the course of the first months.

Aim: To stretch the leg muscles and make them more supple.

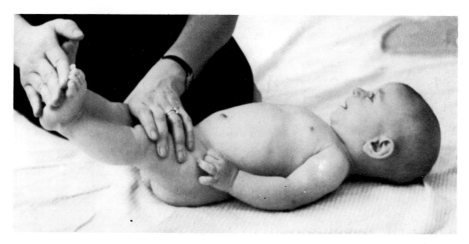

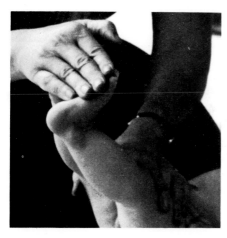

Put one hand under the sole of the feet (ankles at right angles), and the other hand over the knees. Gradually straighten the legs out by moving them up and down without going right down to the ground.

strengthening the thighs

Position: The child flat on his back on the ground or on
the table.

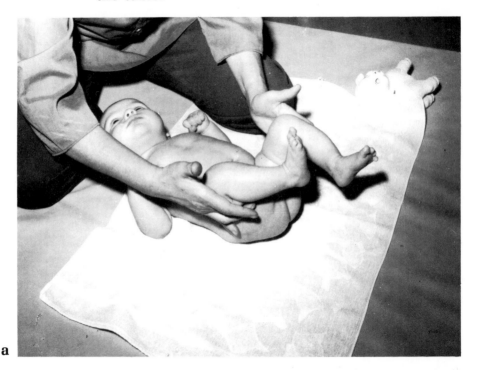

a

With hands cupped behind the child's knees **(a),** by tossing
very slowly and gently, straighten the legs and spread
them apart **(b).**

Note: Never fight against resistance. You must wait until the muscles are relaxed.

Aim: To make the inner muscles of the thigh more supple while stretching them out and relaxing them.

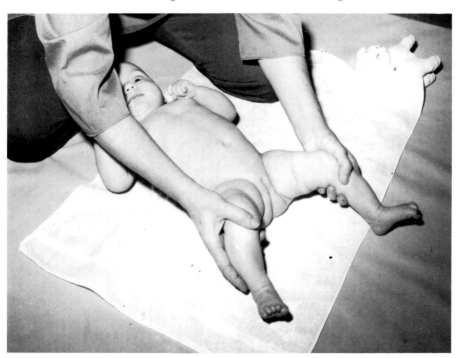

b

game on the roll

Position: On the ground or table, the child lying on his
tummy, arms over the smaller roll (see page 3).

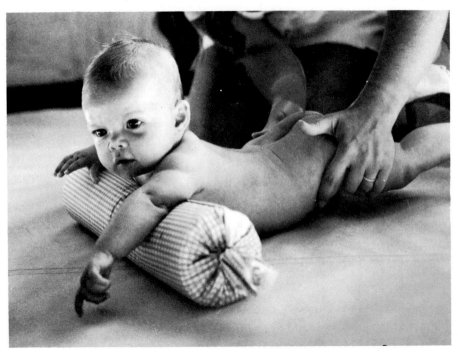

Holding the child by his thighs and pelvis, push him gently
backward and forward. Attract his attention with a toy.

Note: Support the pelvis gently.

Aim: To loosen the arms.

abdominal movements

Position: The child flat on his back on the ground or the table.

Aim: Toning up the abdominal walls.

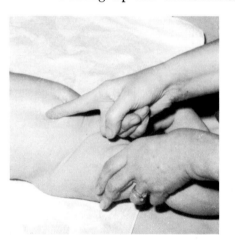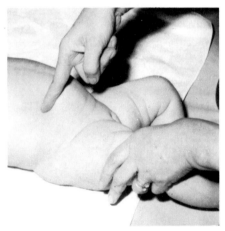

With your nail, trace a series of precise straight lines on the child's stomach, around the navel. With each touch of the nail you should feel the abdomen tightening.

Note: After each stroke, wait for the child's reaction.

Position: The child flat on his back on the ground or the table.

Aim: Regularization of bowel movements. Toning up the abdominal walls.

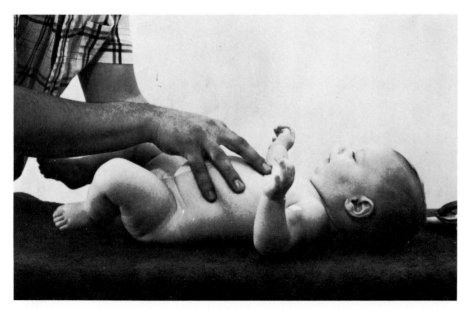

With your whole hand, take hold of the abdomen delicately but firmly. You should feel the child pulling in his tummy: take your hand away immediately. Encourage the child with your voice and movements to get his participation.

Note: Do these exercises four or five times at bathtime. If the child is constipated or has umbilical hernia, five or ten times at each diaper change.

respiratory movements

Position: On the ground or on the table, the child flat on his back, with his knees up.

Aim: Deeper breathing. Use of costal breathing and working the diaphragm.

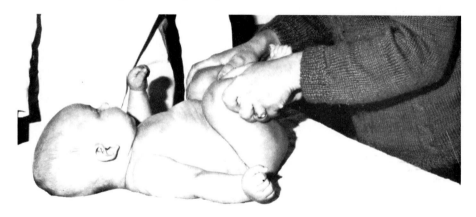

Press the child's knees gently onto his tummy, thus making the abdomen pull in. Wait until the child breathes out fully, then stop pressing. The child will breathe in again. Repeat four or five times.

Note: Do not press the abdomen for more than a few seconds.

Position: The child flat on his back on the ground or on the table.

Aim: To achieve deeper breathing. To avoid pushing the floating ribs out. To make the diaphragm work fully.

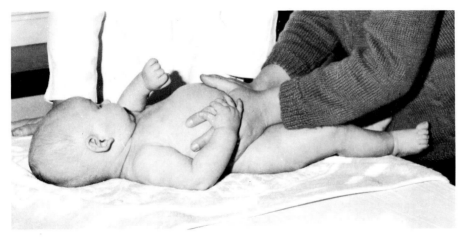

Cup your hands around the child's tummy, holding the base of the rib cage with your fingertips. With your palms, move the abdomen gently up toward the chest, holding the base of the ribs meanwhile. The child will breathe out deeply. Release your hold and he will then breathe in even more more deeply.

Note: The pressure should always be limited.

back movements

Position: The child flat on his tummy on a small tapering cushion on a foam rubber mat (see page 3).

Aim: The toning up of the back muscles. To give the child the opportunity of playing with and feeling the ground with his hands.

The child should lean on his hands or forearms. Stroke the length of his back to make him raise his head and back.

Note: Use a cushion the right size for the child. Make sure his back does not arch.

Position: Hold the child against you, one hand on his knees, the other under his chest. The mirror allows you to check the position of your hands and the reactions of the child.

Aim: The strengthening of the neck and back muscles.

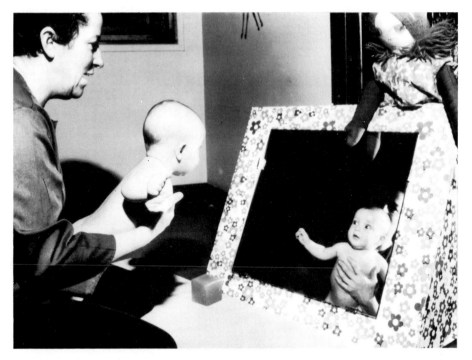

Let the child lean over as far as he can manage. Arouse his interest so that he straightens his back.

turning over and back again

Position: The child flat on his back on a foam rubber mat.

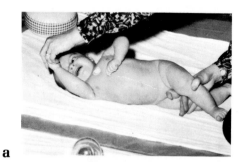

a

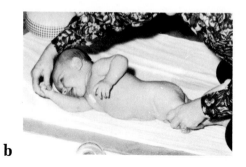

b

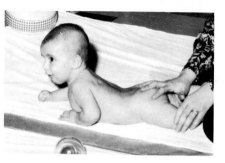

c

Turning over from flat on the back to flat on the stomach.

Cup your right hand under the bent left knee of the child, your wrist keeping the right leg stretched out on the ground **(a).** Flex his left hip, raise his left buttock, rolling him toward the right side. With the left hand, stretch the child's right arm out and upward **(b).** Continue turning him over onto his tummy **(c).** Keep the child interested by patting his bottom or attracting his attention with a toy, and praise him each time he makes an effort.

Note: Try this movement first with the rag doll to get the child perfectly relaxed and reassured. Always keep the hip fully flexed.

Aim: Beginnings of a voluntary movement.

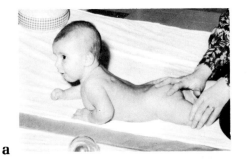

a

b

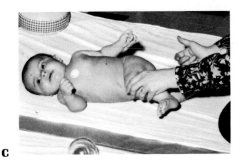

c

Turning over from flat on the stomach to flat on the back. This is much easier. Throw back the child's shoulder by folding his right arm under his chest **(b).** Turning onto the back follows almost automatically **(c).** The first few times, support the child's head so that it does not hit the ground.
Repeat the movement on the other side. Take the child's right knee with your left hand, etc.

SECOND PHASE:
from three to six months

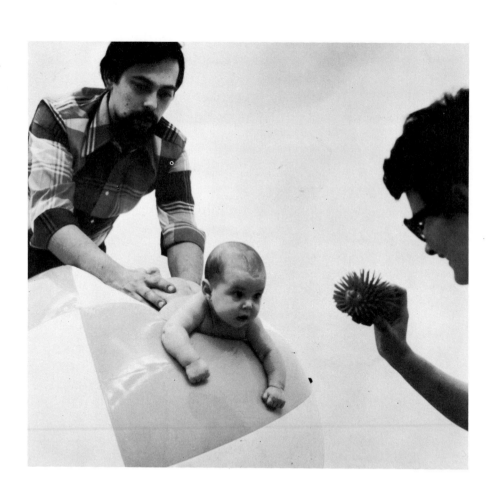

The body grows much less tense, the neck and body muscles more elastic. There are now positive reactions to surroundings: the baby will turn his head toward a noise, look for a human face, use his balancing reflexes, find his bearings in a space, and play with his body then look at his hand; soon he will be able to co-ordinate sight and grasp.

What can you do with your baby?

Relaxing: Passing from one phase to another must be done gradually. Certain movements can be continued for several weeks: for example, continue with the muscle relaxing exercises if the child is still overactive.

Gymnastics: During this phase, gymnastics are important. Their aim is to tone up the muscles in preparation for the sitting position. It is a good idea to alternate dorsal and abdominal movements. The time reserved for this should be limited (ten minutes to a quarter of an hour before or after bathing).

All-round movements: We are no longer concerned with a passive body, but with a child who has his own reactions. He should find his own balance and use necessary supports (your hands, shoulders, and feet, for example) to feel the different positions and discover the reactions of his own body. The exercises involving the whole body can be continued longer if the child is participating actively, without becoming overtired.

What you should know

Use the big beach ball. This is an object which facilitates the search for balance; its volume, suppleness (the ball should be slightly deflated), and firmness reassure the child. Important: The child should be naked.

You must, however, learn to use the ball properly (practice with the big rag doll): you will soon master the technique, and be able to carry out many exercises with ease. Do the exercises in front of a mirror to gain better control. The child should know the different moments of his day—the "ritual"—very well; he will look forward to the gymnastics session following bathtime. No movement should be forced on the child, merely suggested in some way. Encourage active participation, but never insist if he refuses or is tired. All these activities should be for play and shared relaxation. If you enjoy it, he will like the feel of his naked body in your hands.

Advice for day-to-day routine

How should the child be carried? As soon as his muscles are sufficiently developed, you will be able to carry him astride your hip, one hand on his knees and the other on his chest, his face away from you.

How should he be put to bed? The crib should be big, preferably with bars, for the child should be able to look at everything around him. Hang a brightly colored shiny mobile above his crib; he will watch it going around, and babble to it all the time.

How should he be spoken to? The child responds to the sound of voices by moving his eyes and head and then by crying. During gymnastics, repeat the same words and songs for the same movements. Tell the child everything that you are going to do together.

When should he sit? The child may use a comfortable armchair in a semi-lying position; he should be fastened in, as his feet will not be supported by the ground. This should be done only at mealtimes.

How should he be dressed? Dress him in as few clothes as possible; if it is warm enough, just a diaper and a very soft, roomy shirt, allowing him to move as much as he wants, will suffice at first.

Bathtime: The most privileged moment of all. Let the child do just as he wants. Name the different parts of the body as you wash them: "I'm washing your neck, your hair, give me your hand, your foot..." Prompt his participation. Use each spontaneous movement of the child to continue and achieve the necessary one.

Outings: Daily if possible. Take a blanket with you and let the child play freely on the grass.

Toys: His own feet and hands will be his best playthings; also brightly colored cloths, noisy toys, things to bite and suck, squeaky rubber toys, various things to feel—soft, hard, warm, cold, sharp, and rough, and paper to crumple. They should be given only when the child is awake.

Environment: Should be commensurate with child's motor activity and a little above it. During the day, place the child as often as possible on a foam rubber mat on the ground. Disperse the toys around him, and let him move freely.

BACK MOVEMENTS

Note: Watch the position of the pelvis. The lumbar region should be slightly arched at the end of the movement. Always take into account the child's potentialities and never overtire him. These movements are games.

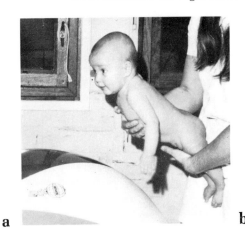

a

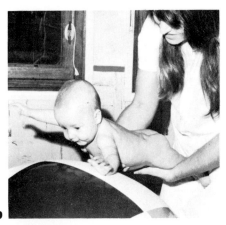

b

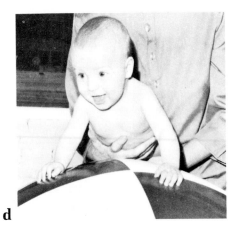

d

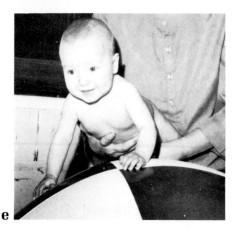

e

Aim: Strengthening the muscles of the neck, back, buttocks, and abdomen.

leaning on the ball

Position: Hold the child against you, one hand on his knees, the other under his chest.

Lean the upper part of the child's body toward the ball **(a),** until he supports himself on it with his hands **(b),** and makes a small effort to raise himself up again **(c).**

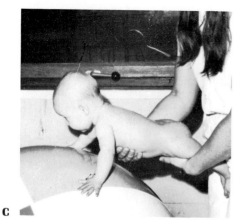

Position: The child leaning on the ball **(d),** held by the thighs and under the thorax.

c

Make the ball roll, thus causing the child to let go of his support with one hand **(e),** and then the other, then both **(f).**

Note: Place your hands so that the hips can move freely.

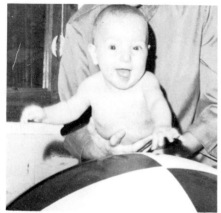

f

on the ball

Position: The child flat on his tummy.

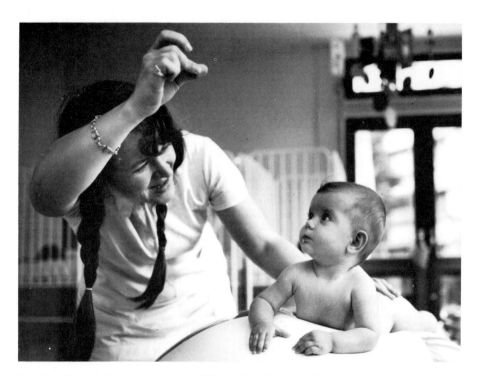

Push the child gently, holding his buttocks, and make the
ball move along while keeping his attention with a toy. He
will raise his head, neck, and back while supporting
himself on his hands.

Position: The child flat on his tummy.

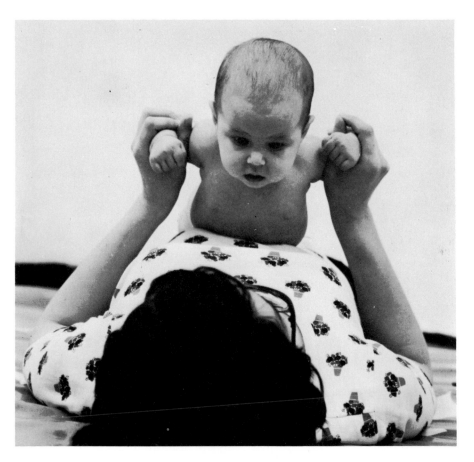

The child will make an effort to lift up his head and back.

dorso-lumbar movements

Position: The child flat on his tummy, head and shoulders
reaching out over the table edge. Increase the
difficulty by moving the child forward until
the upper part of his body is entirely
unsupported.

Aim: Strengthening of the para-vertebral muscles.

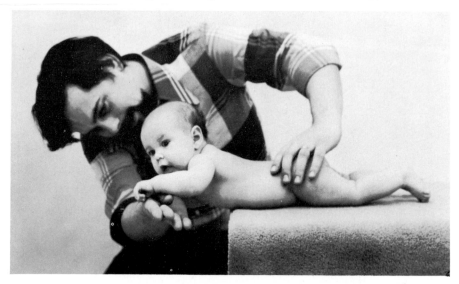

With one hand hold the child's buttocks; with the other,
support him by his forearms. He will raise himself up.
Gradually remove the support from under his arms.

Note: Increase the difficulty in proportion to the child's
muscular development.

Position: The child flat on his tummy, legs over the edge of the table.

Aim: Strengthening of the buttocks and lumbar muscles.

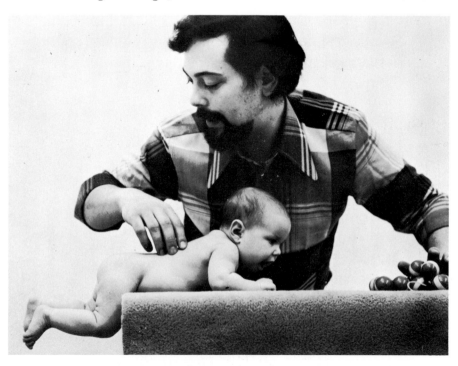

Stimulate the child's buttocks and lumbar region by patting and pinching gently to make the legs stretch out completely.

Note: Watch the position of the pelvis; the lumbar region should be slightly arched, the thighs resting on the edge of the table.

Position: Hold the child with one hand on his knees, the other under his chest. He is in the position to support himself on his hands on the table or ground.

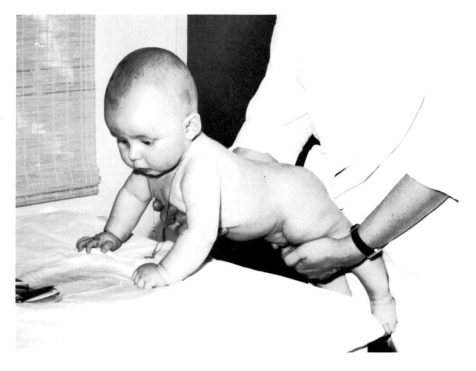

Wait until he holds up his back and neck. Gradually encourage the child to really support himself on his outstretched arms.

Aim: Strengthening the muscles of the neck and back. Strengthening the arms and the pectoral muscles. Development of the rib cage. For deeper breathing.

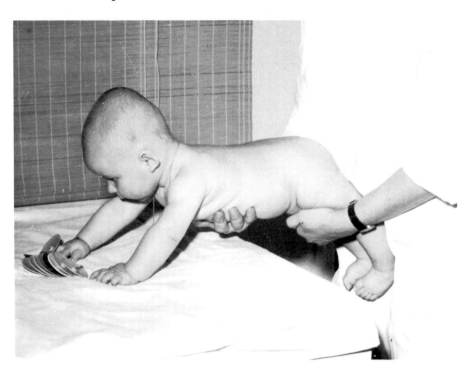

Position: The child on the ground, on his
knees in front of the roll **(a)**.

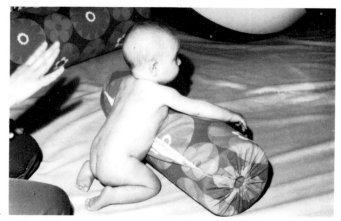

a

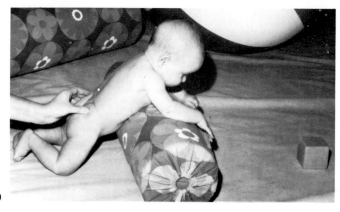

b

Push the child on his stomach across the
roll. Put a toy in front of him. Indicate
the movement that will help him to reach

Note: This is a game. The movement must be made very slowly; give the child time to feel for and gain his balance.

Aim: To reach the desired object. Preparation for all-fours position. Muscle development of the arms and back.

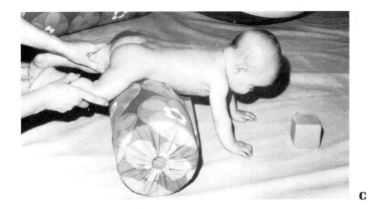

c

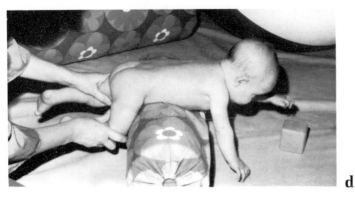

d

it **(d).** Hold him by the knees **(c),** the buttocks **(b),** or the ankles, while rolling him along gently.

ABDOMINAL MOVEMENTS

Note: Watch the position of the lumbar region, which should be entirely in contact with the ground. Take account of the child's capabilities. Do not overtire him.

Aim: Strengthening the muscles of the neck, stomach, and thighs.

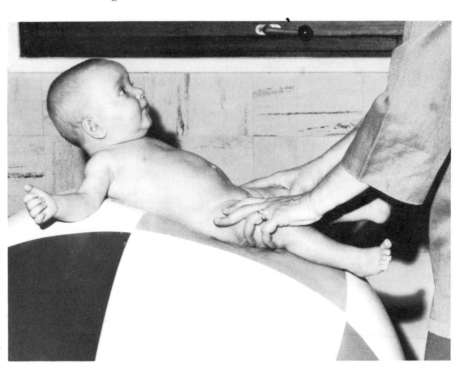

a

Position: The child flat on his back, legs stretched out, held by the thighs **(a).**

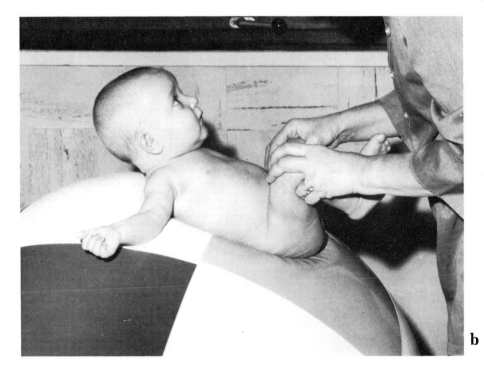

b

While bending up the child's legs, make the ball move from back to front so that he will lift his head away from it **(b).**

Position: The child flat on his back, legs held down, bent
up or stretched out.

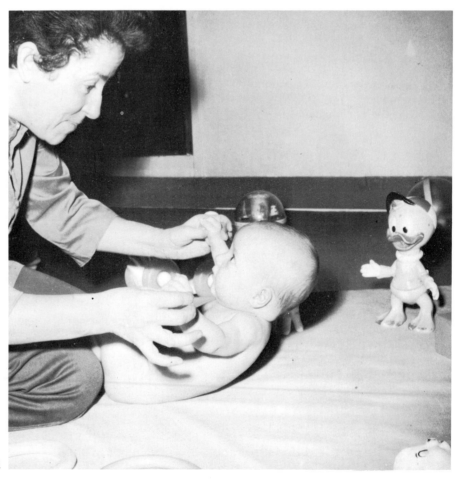

a

a. The child holds your thumbs while you hold down his legs, encouraging him to raise his head and chest toward you.

b. Support the child's head so as to get the same movement.

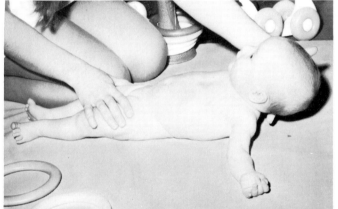

b

c

c. The child raises his head all by himself.

Position: The child flat on his back, arms stretched out
sideways, a toy above his navel.

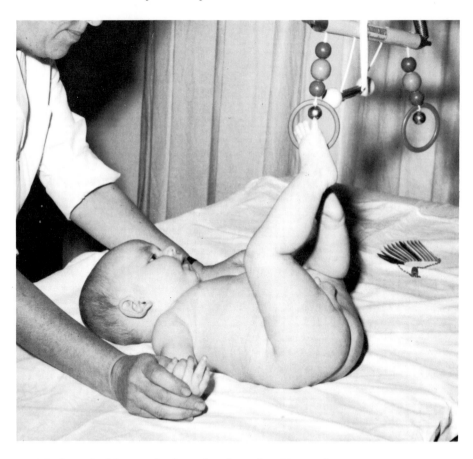

Hold the child gently by the hands. Draw his attention to
the toy, which he will try to get hold of with his feet. Move
the toy further away to increase the difficulty.

lying/sitting on the ball

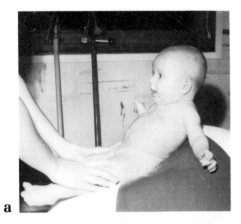

a

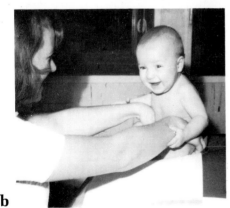

b

Position: The child lying flat on his back on the ball, held down by his thighs **(a).**

Tip the ball slightly and slowly forward, back, to one side, then the other. The child will then be sitting up **(b).**

Aim: Preparing for sitting. Finding his balance.

Note: Do not leave the child in the sitting position. If this movement is beyond his capabilities, wait a while.

Position: The child flat on his back, legs stretched out in front **(a).**

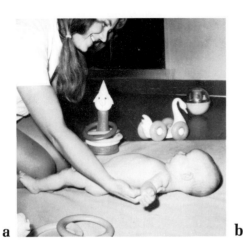
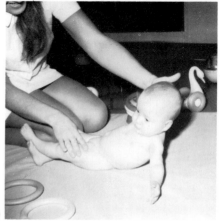

a   b

Hold the child's head and right shoulder up **(b).** Raise him slightly, turning his chest over to the left so that he is resting on his shoulder, elbow **(c),** hand, and then is in the sitting position. Repeat the movement from the other side **(d).**

Aim: Strengthening the abdominal muscles.

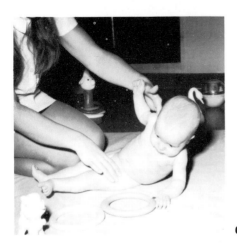 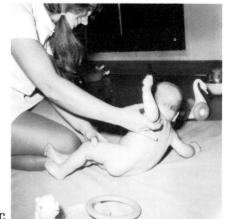

c   d

Position: The child flat on his back on the ball **(a),** or on the ground.

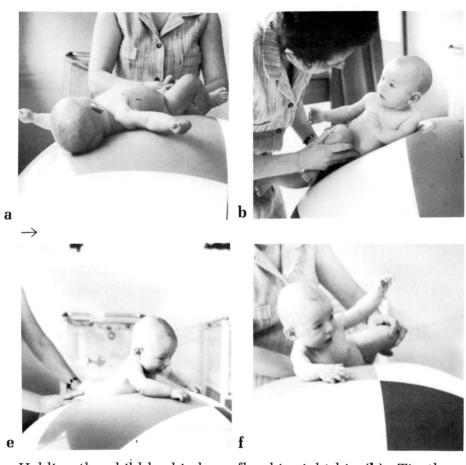

a →

b

e

f

Holding the child by his legs, flex his right hip **(b).** Tip the ball slowly and gently from left to right **(c d),** guiding the child quite naturally to his tummy **(e).**

Note: Watch the flexing of the hip.

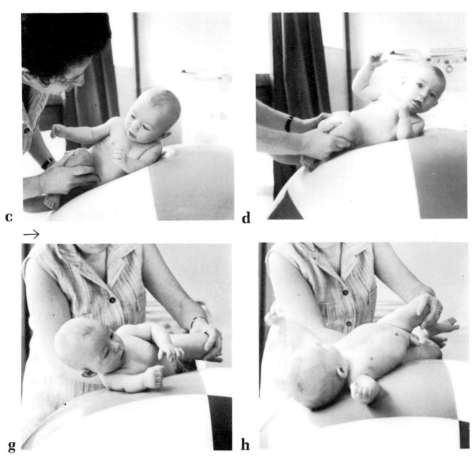

c

→

d

g

h

Repeat the movement, but tip the ball from right to left
(f g), to get the child onto his back **(h).**

Position: The child flat on his back
on the ground.

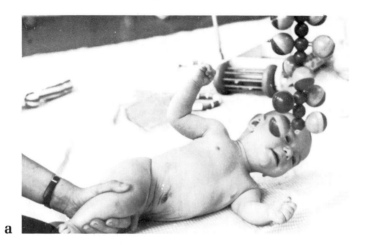

a

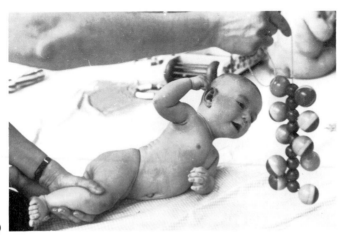

b

Flex the child's right hip **(a)**. Show him
a toy **(b),** while turning him slightly
toward it **(c).** He will then be flat on his
tummy again **(d).** Continue the game,
making him roll over on his own.

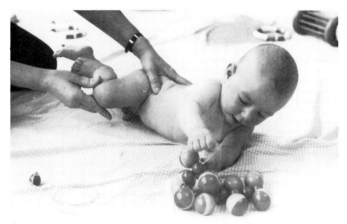

c

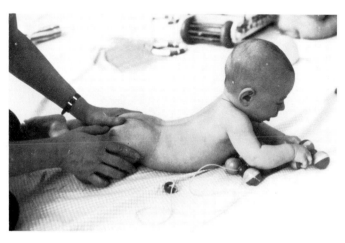

d

THIRD PHASE:
from six to twelve months

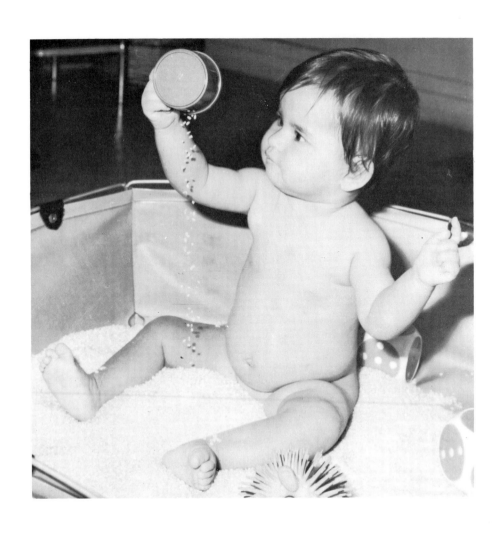

The third and fourth phases overlap. Each child develops at his own speed.

These two phases are often the most productive and happiest for parents and family. The child will begin to imitate and do on his own the movements you have made him aware of.

The child can now use his toys, get hold of them, let them go: grip has been mastered and he will use it a great deal. He can recognize his environment and distinguish between the people around him. He is aware of himself and others. Toward the eighth month the child, very attached to his mother, may be distressed by her absence. This is the period when you must respond to this distress, by making the child feel secure in his own body. His social needs are beginning to assert themselves: crawling may help him to satisfy them.

What can you do with your baby?

Relaxing: Still useful if the child has difficulty going to sleep.

Gymnastics: Gymnastic movements are now fully understood. You must continue with them, gradually increasing their difficulty, being aware of the capabilities of your child. Never insist if the child has no inclination. The time must always be limited to ten minutes.

All-round movements: These are, in fact, simple movements, reproducing those seen in the child's normal development. Easy to do and to link together, they allow him to acquire the reflexes of balancing and righting himself. They are all games that he will use during the course of the day. The games with the ball, the big roll, and the sitting position on a little stool will allow him to become aware of his body. He begins to have control over himself; all these efforts are aimed at leading him to independence.

What you should know

The games should not be continued if the child seems to be losing interest. In fact, it is sufficient to make him feel his capabilities, to put him in the "position," to give him his first chance; later, he will repeat this search on his own. Many games that you will invent will complete the basic exercises.

It must be emphasized again that there is no compulsion for either adult or child. If on some days you cannot play with your child, no matter. During the exercises suggested for this third phase, you will arrive, without noticing it, at the fourth, which is the great discovery, the beginning of true independence, walking unaided.

Advice for day-to-day routine

How should the child be carried? Astride the hip; reduce, and then remove entirely, the support around the chest, as soon as the child's muscular strength permits.

How should he be put to bed? Let him sleep on the foam rubber mat on the ground during the day, leaving the crib for night use. The mat left on the ground will encourage the child to decide, to choose, to go toward his crib when sleepy.

How should he be spoken to? The child will "speak" to attract your attention. His cries will become coos and distinct sounds, and you will "answer"; communication has begun. The child can imitate and repeat easy sounds. He will recognize the names of movements and games. He will answer when his name is called, and so on.

When and how should he sit? The dorsal and abdominal muscles are now very firm, but still the child must feel and find his own balance. We have seen many children who are incapable of sitting acquire this balance after a few minutes of trying the following (cf. p. 80): place a little stool in such a way that the child can put his feet flat on the ground, at right angles to his ankles, knees at right angles to his thighs, hips at right angles to his trunk. Reassure the baby while holding his thighs.

You will see him sitting up straight; gradually lessen your support—he will search for and find on his own the balance that allows him to sit up. You are thus preparing him quite naturally for standing by making him aware of the role played by his feet. From that moment on, you can seat him on a little armchair or a high chair (watch that his feet are always resting on the floor) with a table in front of him to play or eat at.

How should he be dressed? The same recommendations for clothes as previously. For footwear, soft slippers with leather soles so that the child does not slip. Weather permitting, he can be barefoot.

Baths: As soon as the child can sit, teach him to wash himself, naming each part of his body: "Wash your foot, wash your neck." And to dry himself, "Dry your foot, neck, right hand, left hand."

Meals: As soon as the child wishes, let him eat by himself, even if he gets dirty. To teach him to be clean, however, wipe his mouth and hands and then get him to follow your example.

Outings: Put him on the ground, even if he does eat the grass!

Games and toys: Lightweight, brightly colored balls of different size and consistency; big blocks, toys that fit inside each other and interlock, big beads to thread; cups to empty and fill with sand in the yard, rice in the house (be sure to watch the child); a teddy bear, a rag doll that can be dressed in clothes and shoes; a mirror; a big box that can be filled and, more important, emptied; toys to push and pull, tricycles without pedals, a big wagon, a stool on casters, puppets, picture books.

Environment: According to the child's curiosity and abilities.

BACK MOVEMENTS

Note: Watch the position of the pelvis. The lumbar region
should be slightly arched at the end of each
movement. Always take account of the child's
capabilities, never overtire him.

Aim: Strengthening the muscles of the neck, back, and
buttocks. Preparation for sitting and standing
positions.

Position: Hold the child against you, one hand under his knees, the other under his chest.

Lean the child over as far as his strength will allow. Give less support under his chest by gradually lowering your hand. Arouse his interest to make him lift himself up.

game with the snake

Position: Hold the child against your knees. He
will try to catch the snake.

on top of a table

Position: The child on top of a table or on
the ground. Hold the child by
his thighs, then by his knees,
and then his ankles. Make him
go forward on his hands.

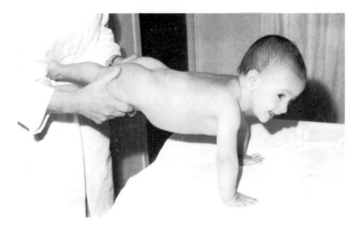

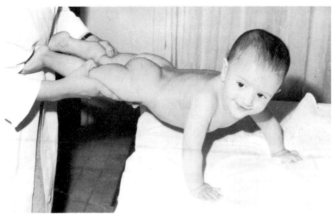

Aim: To develop the pectoral and dorsal
muscles.

on the roll

Position: The child flat on his tummy
along the roll, held lightly by the
legs.

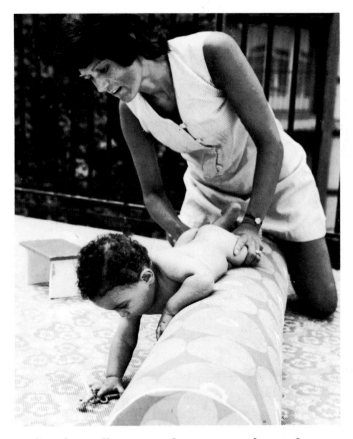

Make the roll tip gently over to the right
and then to the left; this will stimulate an
asymmetrical dorsal contraction and a
consequent search for balance.

game on the roll

Position: The child in front of the roll.

Show the child his favorite toy; encourage him to go and
fetch it. Leave the child on his own to make the necessary
effort to reach the object he wants.

ABDOMINAL MOVEMENTS

on the ground

Position: The child sitting, hold his legs. While you gradually raise his legs, the child will resist the lack of balance for one moment, then allow himself to go on his back.

Note: Never go beyond the child's capabilities.

Aim: To develop the muscles of tummy and thighs.

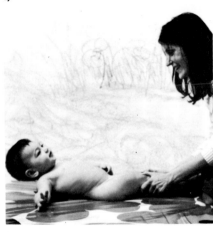

on the roll

Position: The child sitting across the roll, held at the thighs and knees.

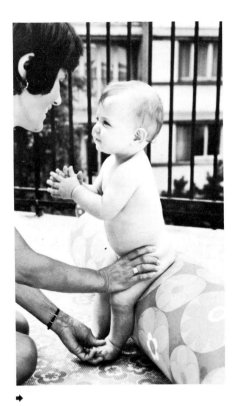 

➡

Move the roll gently from front to back and from back
to front, allowing the child to use his abdominal
muscles and support himself on his feet.

➡

on the ball: seesaw

Position: The child sitting on the ball.

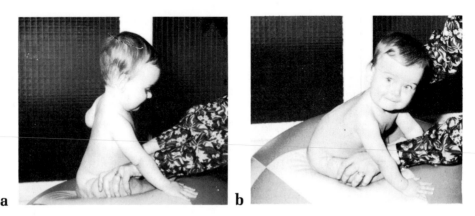

a   b

Sit opposite the child, holding him along his thighs **(a).** Tip
the ball from right to left **(b),** from front to back **(c),** from
back to front **(d).** This lets the child use his abdominal
muscles and find his balance in a sitting position.

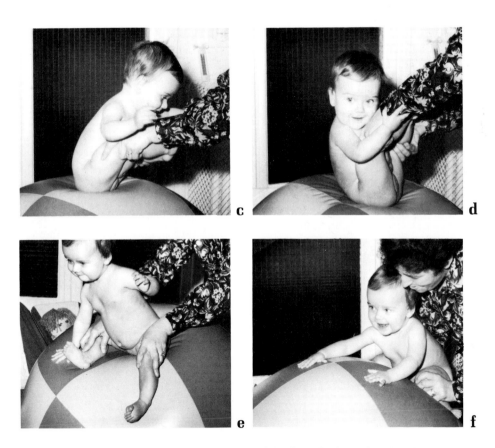

Repeat the game, putting yourself behind the child who is sitting **(e),** or kneeling **(f).**

lying/sitting on the ball

Position: The child lying flat on his back on the ball, held by the thighs **(a)**.

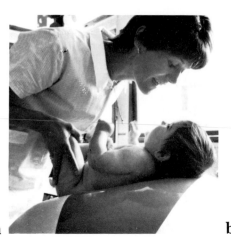

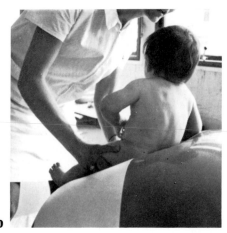

a   b

Roll the ball gradually and gently from front to back, leaning it slightly to the right so that the child will be guided quite naturally into a sitting position, using balancing reflexes. You will see that he is resting first on his shouder, then his elbow **(b),** and finally his hand **(c),** with the arm stretched out. Repeat the movement, leaning the ball over to the left.

The child is now sitting **(d).** Continue to play with the ball, without making the movement jerky. Roll the ball in all directions **(e),** giving the child enough time to adjust to the frequent changes of balance.

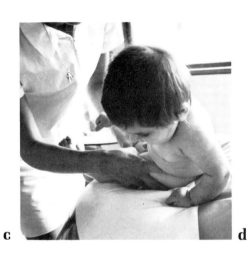

c

d

e

f

lying/sitting on the ground

Position: The child lying flat on his back on the ground, held by his thighs.

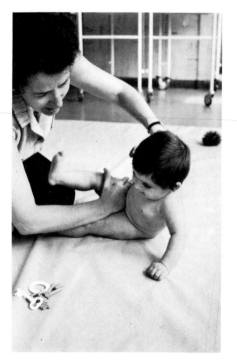 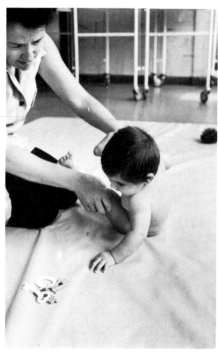

Raise the child's right shoulder (directing the movement over to the left); let him lean on his left shoulder, then on his elbow, then his hand (the left arm being stretched out), until finally he is sitting. To make him lie down again, lean him on his hand, elbow, and left shoulder. Repeat the movement on the other side.

Note: Watch that the child does all that he is capable of, on his own. Do not tire him; be fully aware of his capabilities. Stimulate his interest by putting a toy within his reach.

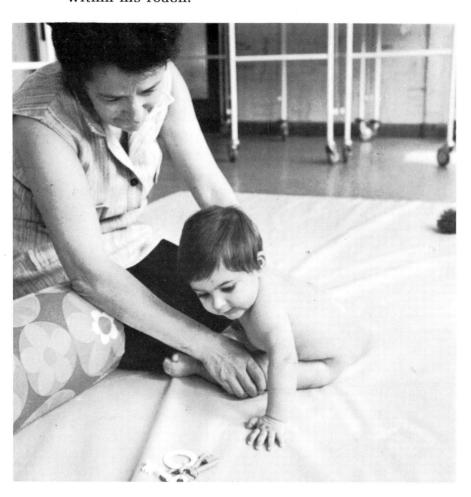

sitting on a stool

Position: The child should be seated on the stool with his feet on the ground, ankles at right angles to the feet, knees at right angles to the thighs, hips at right angles to the trunk.

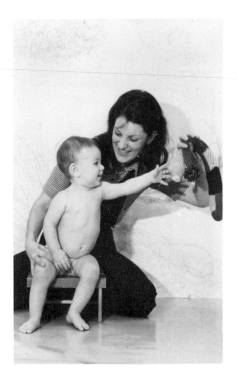 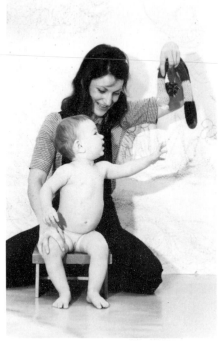

Place yourself behind the child, holding him by one thigh
alone; avoid all support for the back. Give him time to find
and gain his balance. He will straighten his back, turning
from side to side and supporting himself on the ground with
his feet.

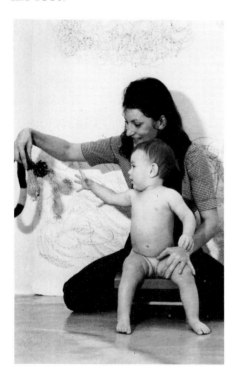

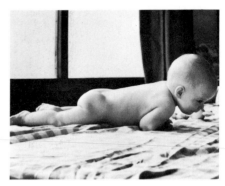

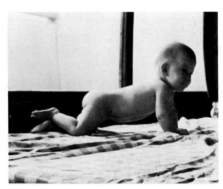

GAMES ON THE ROLL

astride

Position: Both mother and child sitting astride the roll. Hold the child by his thighs or pelvis.

Lean the roll over to the right and then the left, so that the child is putting his weight on one foot and then on the other. Stop between each movement so that the child recognizes the role played by his feet.

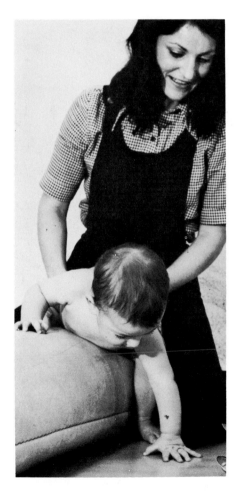 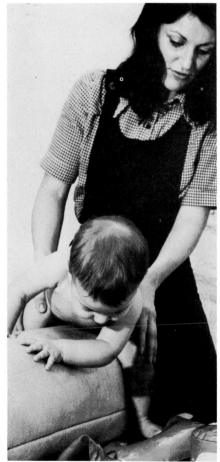

on all fours/kneeling

Position: The child on all fours on the roll
(or on his father's thigh).

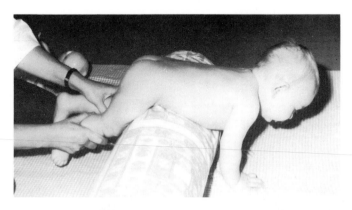

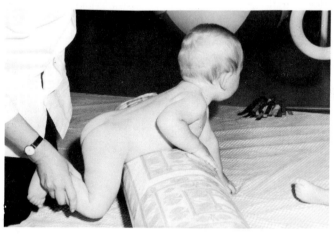

Move the roll slightly from front to back,
making the child lean alternately on his
knees and hands. After a very short time,
he will make active use of his hands and
knees.

Position: The child leans on the roll on all fours, then with arms and legs outstretched.

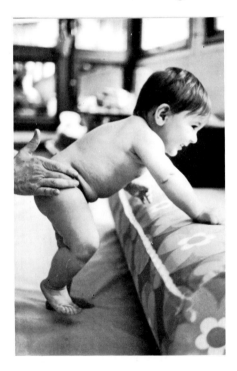 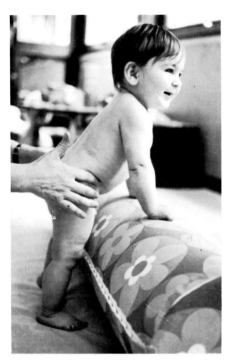

Move the roll so that the child will follow it, leaning on it with his hands, and gradually reaching an erect position.

Position: The child sits across the roll. Hold him by his thighs from the front.

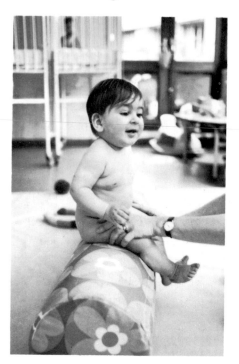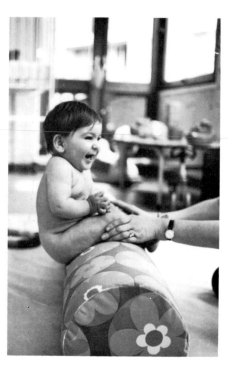

Note: The movement must be done very slowly.

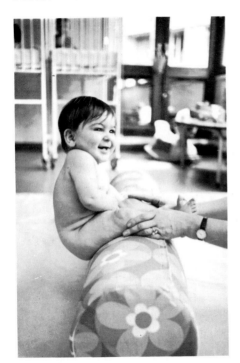 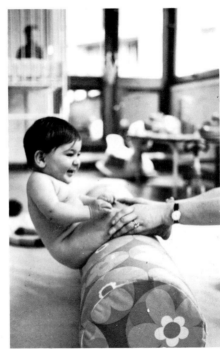

Move the roll backward, then forward. The child will try to struggle against loss of balance.

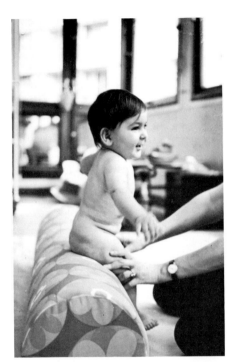 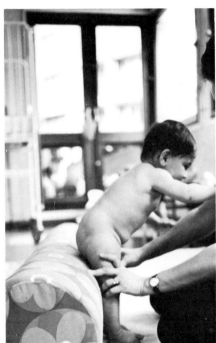

The child will pass naturally from the sitting to the standing position.

FOURTH PHASE:
from nine to fifteen months and beyond

This is the age when the child gets real pleasure from being able to move. He will want to reach everything, have everything, do things by himself. However, he needs your loving presence for stimulation and reassurance, so that he can make progress. This is the age of shared pleasure.

What can you do with your baby?

Gymnastics: At this period continue gymnastics only if it seems necessary (if there is insufficient muscle development).

All-round movements: These will be games, which totally involve the child. Never force anything; once again it is a question of giving the idea of the movement, consolidating former skills, and making new ones possible. This becomes real child's play if an attentive hand is present when the child is ready, to help him, give him security, let him become aware of himself, in short, gain self-control. Once again, this is not a question of producing precocious babies, but of making children at home in their bodies. We therefore do away with the awkward period when one sees the child's tummy out, buttocks in the air, only precariously balanced, the strongest group of muscles dominating the weakest, opening the door to the development of various spinal disorders. We give the child the chance, at each new step, to position his body and use his muscles in harmony.

Various objects such as rods, the hoop, and the baby-walker allow the child to free himself from the adult's hand, and from support that is too direct.

What you should know

To see your child standing for the first time is your privilege.
You will be there, your hands placed on his hips, supporting your child's body. From the easing of his body you will sense that he has found his balance. His expression and his mischievous smile will convey to you that he has discovered something wonderful. The next moment, he will try his first step —his, not one that the adult has imposed on him, but one that he can and wants to make.
The joy and pride of your child at each new skill will be evident.
His anxious, inquiring glances, then his reassured and finally quite happy looks, will be most rewarding.

Advice for day-to-day routine

How should he be spoken to? The child should now have some understanding. He will respond to instructions such as, "Open your mouth, give me your hand, go and find your toy." Use washing and dressing times, mealtimes, and walks to point out, with the aid of simple but exact words, pictures, toys, people, and acts of daily life.

Bathtime: The child should be able to wash almost entirely by himself.

Clothes: Always use simple clothes. The child may begin to dress himself. Your patience now will save you time later on, but most important, you will be helping your child once more to gain his independence. Shoes should be soft; arch supports are necessary only on medical advice. Walking barefoot is the best solution, if this is at all possible.

Meals: Leave him to feed himself. Give him a spoon, later on, a fork; at first there will be a great deal of mess, but you will gradually be able to teach him to eat neatly.

Toilet training: None before fifteen to eighteen months.

Outings, Environment: Put the child with other children, in the yard, in the sandbox. Leave him free to experiment. Make him walk on different types of ground.

Games: Sliding on sleds, climbing ladders, going down stairs, rolling down hillsides, falling, getting up, and so on.

sitting/crawling

Position: The child seated on the ground, legs slightly
apart **(a).** Put his favorite toys within his reach.

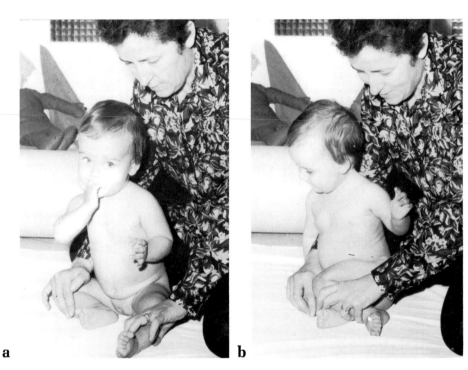

a   b

Bring the child's right foot up against his left thigh, bend
the left leg over the right **(b).** With your left hand, hold
both his ankles and with your right (passed under his arms)
hold the child under his left arm **(c).**

Aim: To allow the child to move or to reach the desired
object.

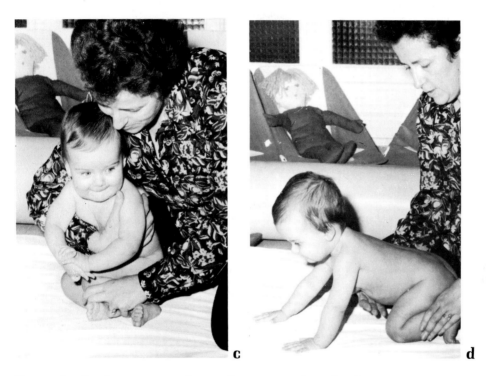

c   d

Turn the body over to the right to get the child onto all
fours **(d).** Repeat this movement from the other side—that
is, bringing the left foot up against the right thigh, etc.

Position: The child on all fours on the ground **(a).**

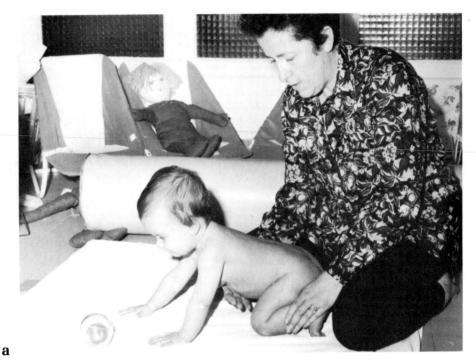

a

Bring the child's buttocks down onto his heels, with the upper part of his body erect **(b).** Show him a toy at shoulder level so that he turns from one side to the other.

Aim: To allow the trunk to become independent of the legs.

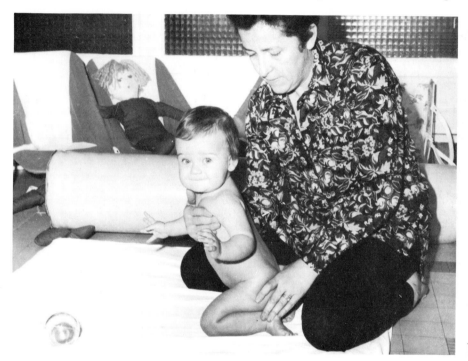

b

little rabbit
crouching/standing

Position: The child sitting on his heels, the upper part of his body erect.

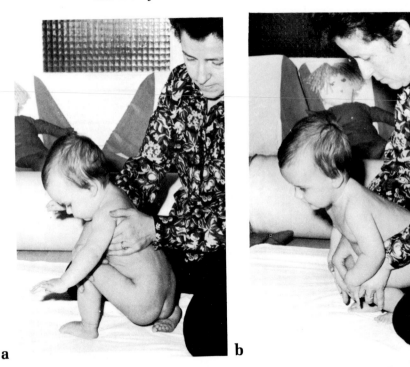

a   b

Put one of his legs forward, feet flat on the ground, while holding him under his arms **(a).** Bring the other leg up, feet flat on the ground: the child is now in a crouching position. Move him like a seesaw from back to front **(b).** One day he will stand on his feet **(c).**

The day when the child gets up on his feet, he may lurch backward, but on his toes, his heels rising from the ground. This is a very important moment, and the instinctive movement must not be encouraged. Repeat the movement from the crouching position. Hold the child around the knees, swaying him forward so that the weight of the body is carried on the front of the feet. Hold both knees with one hand, the other being on the chest to help the child in his movement toward the standing position. Take care that the weight of the body is always projected forward, and that the lumbar region is slightly arched.

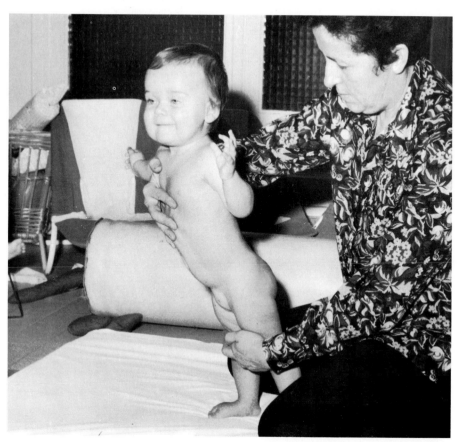

c

GAMES ON THE BABY-WALKER

on all fours/standing

Position: Child on all fours. He will stand up with the help of
the baby-walker.

➡

sitting/standing

Position: The child sitting on a low chair, lightly held under the chest or pelvis.

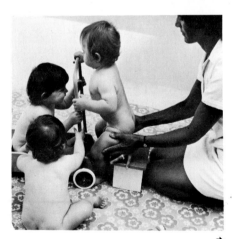

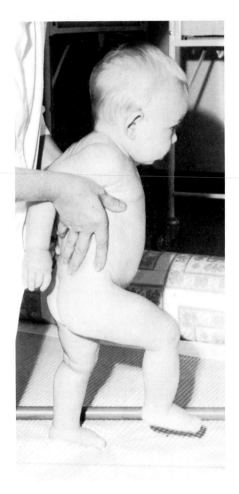 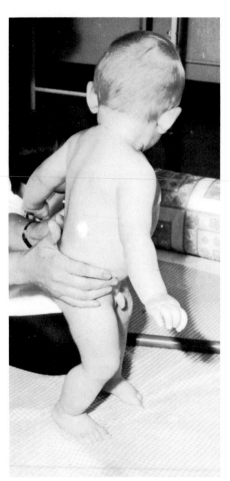

When the child first stands up, leave him to the pleasure of this new sensation. Hold him either by the pelvis or by the loins. Make him turn the upper part of his body to one side, then the other, feet flat on the ground, body leaning slightly

forward. You must feel that the child has understood his
discovery and familiarized himself with this new skill.
Often, in the moment that follows this discovery, the child
supported in this way takes his first step.

the rods

Position: The child standing between the rods.

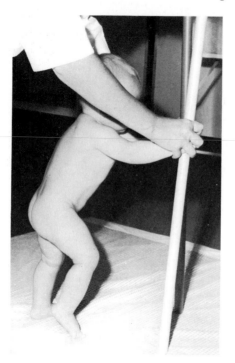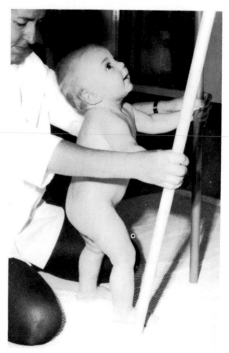

Make the child hold the rods; from behind him put your
hands on his, and move him forward and backward very
gently so as not to frighten him. Then move your hands
above his. Repeat the movement. As soon as the child is

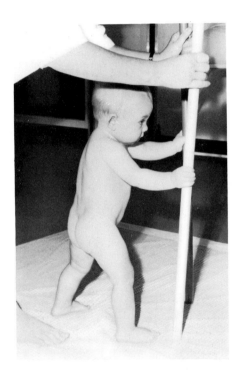 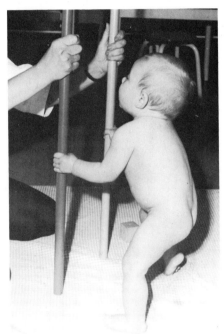

confident, lean the rods forward and the child will take a
step. Try the following movements: move the two rods
forward, then back; move them to one side, then the other;
put yourself in front of the child, then to one side.

the hoop

Position: Face the child; both hold the hoop with two
hands.

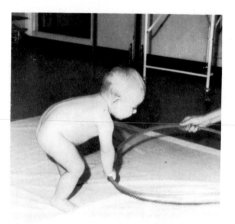

a

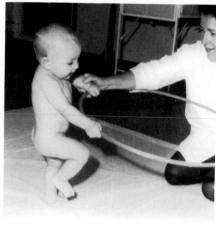

b

Go around in a circle;
make the child step forward, back,
sideways, first in a crouching
position, then standing.

c

Try an accompaniment of songs or a rhythmic beat.

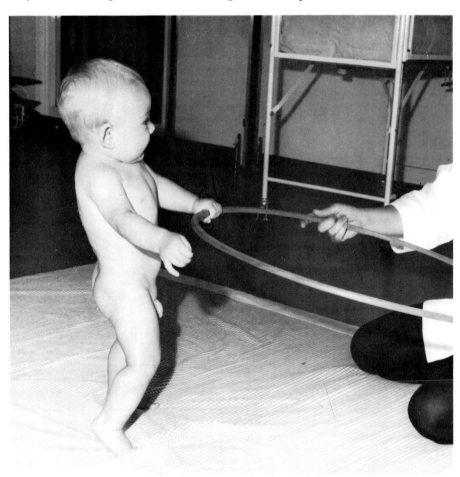

d

a

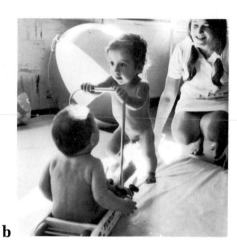

b

e

Let the child make his own decisions and take his own time.
One day you will see him coming toward you or going
straight ahead, calmly and naturally, proud and happy.

c

d

f

g

THE ESSENCE OF OUR PROGRAM

the free child

**sitting without support,
feet resting
on the ground**

trunk rotation

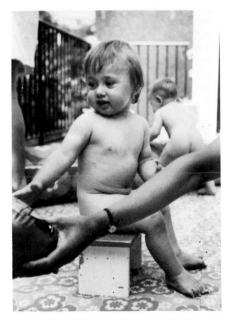

developing standing balance

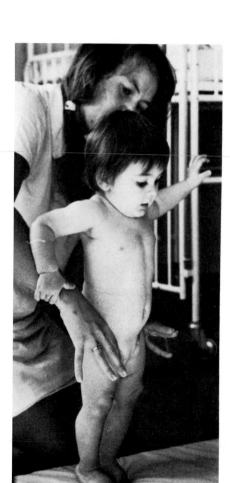
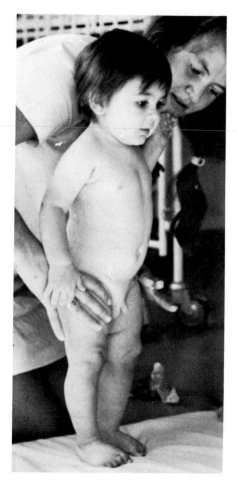

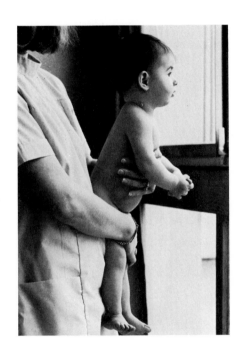
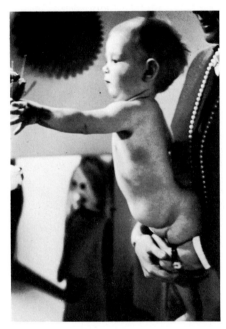

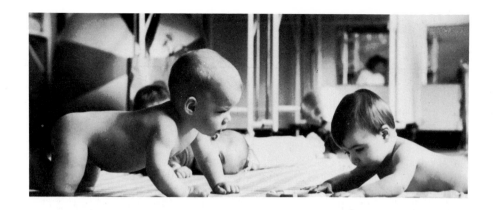

children's games

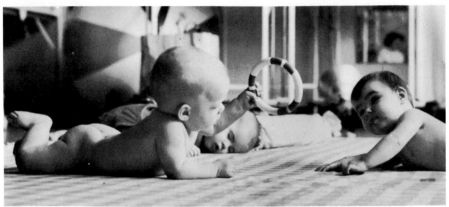

at the day care center

first
step

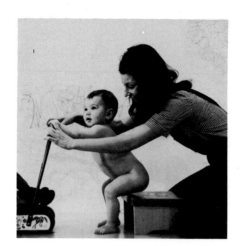

the beginning of another story

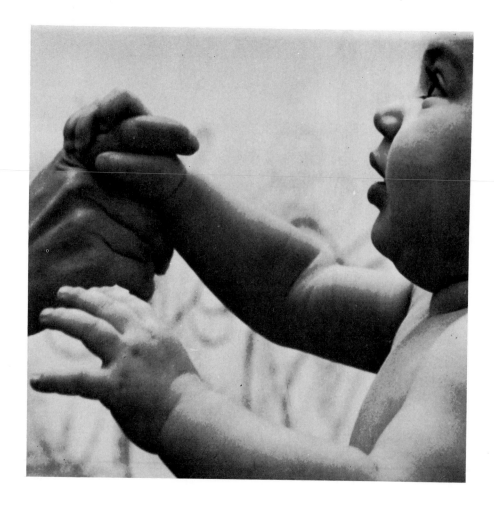